Love After Heartbreak:

How to Bounce Back Emotionally, Trust and Love Again

An encouraging guide for love after breakup and divorce.

By Vishnu of Vishnu's Virtues

*"If you were born with the weakness to fall
you were born with the strength to rise."*

Rupi Kaur

For weekly posts on new beginnings + a video on how to bounce back from rock bottom, sign up at www.vishnusvirtues.com.

Contents

Introduction

I didn't want a divorce.

Although my marriage had many ups and downs, it would have been so much easier to stay in it than to end it. And even though I threatened divorce many times in my marriage, at my core I don't believe I wanted one. Yes, unfortunately, I ended plenty of arguments by saying we should get a "divorce". I was silly and childish when I didn't get my way, so I made these threats.

I say I didn't want a divorce but all my actions and the way I showed up in my marriage created the recipe for divorce. If you want a divorce, be emotionally unavailable, don't work on yourself, never compromise, let your ego rule the relationship and always try to win. Don't forgive easily, hold lots of grudges and use the silent treatment on your partner. Make major financial decisions on your own, and keep your partner guessing about finances and your shaky career plans.

Looking back, I have no words for my actions. I have no idea why I acted the way I did. I can blame it on immaturity, irresponsibility or just not knowing better but it really doesn't matter why I was the way I was. There's no point in rationalizing or justifying my actions. Instead, I choose to look back at the relationship and now I can clearly see where I blundered. I can see where I lost my way and how lousy I was as a partner.

During my divorce in 2011, I vowed I would never love or look for someone again. For years, I believed I had royally screwed up my relationship and was responsible for causing pain. I also believed my heart was broken beyond repair. I felt more ashamed than ever before. I felt worn out, frustrated, hurt and hopeless. I vowed it would be my last relationship and I wallowed in that place for several years.

To be fair, I do know it wasn't 100 percent my fault but it sure did feel that way. It takes two people to make a relationship work and two people to make a relationship fail. I can't speak for my ex and I don't plan to blame her here for any of her shortcomings. I can take responsibility only for my part and speak from my perspective. Also, this book isn't about looking backward – about what went wrong or what happened in the past. It's about moving past our hurts, healing our hearts and finding the courage to love again.

For the past five years, I've been doing a lot of work to understand myself better, to become emotionally stronger and a better version of myself. During that time, I've also become a better partner for a future relationship. The therapy, self-reflection, introspection, coaching and hard liquor has paid off! I'm kidding about the last part but I am not kidding about the changes I've made in my life.

This journey hasn't been easy. The journey after divorce and heartbreak is especially hard because after one serious rejection or broken relationship you begin to think it's a permanent condition. You feel you're unwanted, undesirable or unworthy. You don't think you can ever give or receive love again. You take every rejection and failed relationship as a sign you're not going to find love in the future.

You probably have many questions. I will be the first to tell you that I don't have all the answers. I'm no love guru, love doctor or therapist. I don't have specialized knowledge about love and relationships. In fact, I am probably an expert on how to do it all wrong. All I have for you is my failures and trip-ups but through them I've grown and learned. This book is my attempt to share with you what I've learned on my journey back from heartbreak and divorce.

I hope it will inspire you to do the necessary work, break through the obstacles to love and let yourself open your heart again to another person. The past is the past; the future is in your hands. You might not be able to undo what you've done or do much with the pain you caused but you can show up better next time around.

This book is for you if you're scared of or doubtful about love. It's a book to give you encouragement if you're terrified of love or loving. It's a guide if you're afraid to trust or commit again. It's a strategy book with tools and inspiration to help you move forward in love.

I hope this book gives you hope, insight and guidance to find love, joy and fulfillment in your life.

In friendship,

Vishnu

Chapter 1. Why should you love again and stay hopeful?

Give love another chance but this time around, don't let your love for another person consume you. Don't put all your hopes and dreams into another person. A mature love involves finding the love within yourself, being complete in who you are and only then seeking a partner to fulfill you. It's not the love you hear about in love stories and romance novels.

Society tells you that two halves make a whole. I disagree. You're each one person and you're each whole but together you two are a stronger and more supportive unit. Two people are stronger than one. A life partner will give you emotional and mental support to deal with life's challenges. A partner will give you companionship and friendship.

You should love again because love makes us better people. You likely haven't learned as much by yourself as you did from your last long-term relationship. You likely got a Ph.D. from the relationship, learning about yourself and your partner. Our partners can be mirrors of ourselves; they show us exactly who we are. They provoke us, bother us, hit our pain points and cause us to examine every part of ourselves – the good and the bad, the healthy and the unhealthy. With awareness, our partners cause us to wake up and make changes within.

A good relationship is one in which you and your partner see each other's essence. You let go of the ego, the differences, the conflicts and realize that at the end of the day you're two souls united and traveling through life together. A relationship that works is sacred. It unleashes the divine within you. Some people find the divine in the temple but you can also find it in sipping a cup of tea with someone who cares for you. You can find it in love, romance and strong relationships.

Love requires you to give, to let go and be present for another person. In giving your love, you brighten someone else's life. You extend kindness, you feel gratitude. You receive joy and happiness in your partnership. You may have felt joy and happiness in past relationships. At least you experienced it while dating or before the fights started.

The best part today is that you're not stuck, like many people are, in a dysfunctional relationship that's going anywhere. You have the gift of having ended a relationship that didn't work so you could take another shot at love. You aren't basking in hopelessness and a dysfunctional partnership isn't imprisoning you. You have choices, you have opportunities, you have freedom to create a new relationship from scratch.

You've remained hopeful in other parts of your life and it's always worked. If you were resilient in your school days, you likely achieved your dreams and got the degree you wanted. If you persisted in sports while growing up, you likely won games and competed further. If you survived a health scare, you stood strong and prevailed in the face of disease or death. If you've been hopeful in other areas of your life, why not be hopeful about love? If things have worked out in other areas, why not this one too?

Finally, why should you stay hopeful about the right partner showing up? You've experienced pain, loneliness, struggle and hardship. I believe the world we live in works in cycles and balances itself. I believe if you've suffered and have gone through a season of pain, changes are coming. Happiness comes after pain. Spring comes after winter. Just as easily as you went through pain and hardship, joy and happiness are around the corner.

Stay open, hopeful and welcoming of love. You don't have to sit on the front porch waiting for it to show up. You can simply leave the light on for it and welcome love in when it knocks. Your heart will be thankful for your patience, your positivity and your hope.

Chapter 2. How do you heal the pain from your last relationship?

To move on, you must work on getting over your last relationship. Getting over your last relationship doesn't simply mean the person is no longer in your life, you don't think about the person anymore or you're over the relationship's heartbreak. Often, without knowing it, you are holding onto the pain, betrayal or rejection.

Unlike what many people say, it's not just time that will heal your heart. Time doesn't do anything except maybe make things worse. Your hurt from your past relationship is like an unhealed wound. It won't get any worse over time but it will fester with pain. If you want to move on once and for all, you must get underneath the wound to fully heal it.

I feel like I'm an expert on this topic of not healing from pain. First, let me tell you, being more sensitive towards and resistant to change, for a couple years I could not accept the fact that my relationship was over. I couldn't heal from it. I feel like I can talk to you about pain because I felt the complete depths of pain, danced with it and had to really get to the roots of it to figure out how I could let it go. I mastered grieving, went through intense therapy with three therapists and have come out on the other side. I later realized what I was doing for years was something called rumination; I continued to replay my pain and suffering over and over, emotionally and psychologically.

Whether it is rumination or just plain grief, how do you heal the pain of heartbreak? You cannot move on until you let go of the trespasses your ex committed against you. If you get angry by thinking about all the ways your ex hurt you and how he wronged you, you will be holding onto pent-up hurt and animosity. You must use whatever tools are at your disposal to let go of the hurt.

First, set an intention to forgive your ex and repeat this intention daily. Write a poem, affirmation or quote about forgiveness and look at it every day. Try to put yourself in his shoes and, if possible, empathize with his actions. You don't have to justify those actions but try to understand where he was coming from and all the things that might have led him to behave the way he did. If that doesn't work, use every emotional and spiritual tool available to choose the high road to forgiveness. What would Jesus do? What would the divine of your faith do? What would God want you to do? What would be the highest good of the universe?

If you're having a difficult time getting to forgiveness, you may have to go through the grieving process. It is a process of unwinding all the internal pain and hurt residing in you. To process the pain inside, you must be willing to put a spotlight on it and examine it. This takes work and maybe therapy. You must get to the hurt, understand the emotions you're experiencing and be willing to speak it out. You must be able to share it with someone you trust or with a professional. Only once you get it out there can you do something about it. If you resist and hide your emotions, you won't know why you're upset, whether you're angry or not and what you're angry about.

To completely release the pain and move on, think about the ways this relationship made you a better person. Although challenging, think about how you changed as a person, how your life improved and what were the lessons you learned. You might not believe there was any good that came out of the relationship but if your life is better or has improved in any way, take note of it. Express thanks for your children, for shared memories and for the support you gave each other in achieving your dreams.

After going through this period of mourning and grieving, you might still not want to let go. The biggest struggle many of us face is that we refuse to accept new circumstances and situations. We would rather metaphorically "die" than accept change of any sort. Your resistance to moving on could be your resistance to change. You would rather hold onto a dearly dysfunctional completed relationship than think about any future ones. To help you overcome this fear of change, please remember that bad things happen so that good can come out of them. Rebuilding comes after destruction. Birth comes after death. Renewal comes after deterioration.

To move forward, you must be willing to make friends with change. You must welcome change, see the positivity your new relationship brings and celebrate what's coming up ahead. Your life isn't over; it's just different. You don't have to accept a new "norm", maybe just a different "norm". You embrace change by continuously reminding yourself that life is temporary and good things come with the bad. Remind yourself of all the positive things that will come out of your singlehood; all the benefits of ending a bad relationship. Also, consider the self-awareness and growth you're going to achieve. You might never ask for growth but with life's twists and turns, you can't help but get a little excited about the clarity and insight you're receiving.

Finally, the way to let go once and for all is to tell yourself a new story about this relationship. Sure, you can hold onto the story of pain and heartbreak. You can hold onto the story of betrayal and destruction but it's up to you. Can you tell yourself a different and more empowering story of the relationship? Instead of, *he cheated me out of the life I had and broke my trust in love and relationships,* why not a story of, *he did the best he could, taught me the most I could learn myself and has prepared me for the next chapter of my life.* In any situation, we can tell two stories. You have the power in your mind and heart to tell a more empowering story. A new story to heal your heart and help you move forward.

Chapter 3. How do you overcome feelings of being "not good enough" and build up your confidence?

After forgiving and healing, you're still not quite done with your work if you have feelings of unworthiness or not being good enough. If you're the person who suffered rejection or cheating in the relationship, you're going to have to do a little more work. If you weren't the one who initiated the divorce or the breakup, you're going to feel like you did something wrong. You'll marinate in the world of unworthiness and feelings of not being enough for your partner. *If I wasn't good enough for him, why would anyone else want me?* might be the thought bombarding your mind.

The first step to dealing with these thoughts is to notice and become aware of them. These thoughts may not be readily available to you. They may hide behind your actions. You might not even realize you have feelings of unworthiness. However, these feelings are there if you are afraid of approaching someone, if you're wondering whether someone will like you, if you're thinking you're not good enough for someone. These feelings will prevent you from expressing interest in someone, make you withdraw from a perfectly good relationship and make you go nuts if someone doesn't show interest in you.

Try to catch your thoughts. Make note of these feelings of unworthiness in your body. If you're not sure whether your thoughts demonstrate unworthiness, write down the experiences you have when dating or meeting people. If different thoughts and feelings trigger shame or unworthiness, write them down and try to get to the bottom of them.

One effective technique is to become aware of where these thoughts come from. Give your inner critic a name. Give your critical voice a personality and image so you know who is popping up when negativity flashes through your mind. If you can call out this internal critic by giving it a name, you'll be much more conscious of your thoughts. Your inner "Simon Cowell" or "Donald Trump" is the voice that sabotages you. These voices come out when you're about to take big actions in your life, when you confront your fears or when you decide to take risks. Identifying an image of this internal voice will help you get more clarity when you hear internal voices stemming from fear, doubt or uncertainty.

To work past this internal saboteur, you must be more aware of it and be ready for it when it shows up. Recognizing your internal negative voice helps reduce the power it has over you. In addition to awareness, you must be willing to look within and cultivate love for yourself. You must generate love, acceptance and compassion for yourself. One technique to do this is to think of yourself as a child and speak to yourself like you would to a child who doesn't feel loved. Instead of berating the child and telling the child he/she is unworthy, what would you do? Speak to your inner child this way. Show compassion and understanding when things go south or when you try to blame yourself for actions you take. Do kind things for the benefit of this inner child. Relax, stress less, sleep and help soothe this inner child. Love yourself like you would love a small child.

How you love one person is how you love everyone. You don't have feelings of love towards just a significant other. To get back into the habit of loving, work on loving the people who are most difficult to love. Try to love the people you don't make time for or whom you've taken for granted in your life. Love the people who hurt you or don't treat you very well. Make efforts to improve the way you love the other people in your life and use this as practice for being able to love yourself and, ultimately, someone else. While you're practicing giving love, also be willing to accept love from others. When others do nice things for you or say nice things to you, don't resist or reject their good wishes. Try to stop yourself from rejecting love; instead, practice receiving love.

To boost your feelings of worthiness and your confidence, remind yourself of your good qualities, characteristics and abilities – of how wonderful you are. Imagine if you were toasting yourself at a wedding. What are all the nice things you would say to yourself? What are the things people have said to you at work and in your family? What qualities do people admire in you and look up to you for?

It may be worth your time to write down these positive qualities so you can reflect on these compliments and praises daily. If your inner self is going to knock you down and make you feel unworthy, you might as well challenge these unhelpful thoughts and feelings. You can counter the negativity with a boost of proactive positivity. Use positive images of yourself, reflections on your admirable qualities and affirmations to boost your feelings about yourself.

You're not going to let how one person made you feel take precedence over the reactions of dozens of other people in your life. The only person who brought you down was someone you might not have been compatible with and from who, from a place of ignorance or fear, was trying to hurt you. You don't have to let one person's behavior and actions towards you cloud your image of yourself. You don't have to give him the power to do that. Just because one person hurt or rejected you doesn't mean everyone else is going to do the same.

Another simple way to boost your feelings of self-worth is to surround yourself with people who are supportive, kind and loving towards you. Look at the people in your active social circle to weed out those who harm your self-worth. You can actively make choices to spend less time with others who bring you down.

Finally, feelings of self-worth can increase when you do things that make you feel good about yourself. If you are a great cook, cook more. If you're a writer, write more. If you are a great leader at work, lead more. Whatever it is you do in life that boosts the feelings of worthiness and joy within you, spend more time doing it.

My overall recipe for boosting your confidence and improving your image of yourself is to take a holistic approach. Stay in a positive place where you are working on your thoughts, feelings and actions. Be wary of people and unhelpful thoughts. Cut out the things in your life that negatively affect your self-worth and, instead, work actively on boosting your self-worth each day.

Chapter 4. How do you build yourself up emotionally to love again?

To enter a new relationship, you must build up both your self-worth and your emotional worth. If relationships crush you emotionally and you can't foresee yourself being able to take on another one because you don't think you're emotionally up for it, it's time to work on that.

After your breakup or divorce you likely came out of an emotional hurricane. You have no idea how to bounce back emotionally after the shredding of every single emotion. You might lack the energy, motivation or know-how to rebuild your emotional life.

I have a lot to say about this topic because I was certainly emotionally crushed after my divorce. I'm in a slightly different place today and I'm going to let you in on a secret. I actually feel like I've bounced back quite a bit and am emotionally stronger than ever! Why? Because I hit the lowest of the low and the rockiest of the rock bottom. If you can come back from complete emotional chaos and your entire internal life falling apart, imagine how strong you must be. Life threw the hardest punch at me and, like you, I'm still here and still standing.

To bounce back emotionally, you must feel your emotions completely. A therapist helped me with this and can likely help you uncover, discover and examine the emotional coals burning within you. If you don't examine the emotions, they will continue to burn a hole in your heart. Know what these emotions are. As painful as they may be, you must process them and make space for them. If you want to heal emotionally, you cannot resist your emotions and keep them out of your life. Allow yourself to feel the depth and intensity of your emotions like strong waves rolling onto the beach. The good news is, like waves, emotions recede and go back with the tide.

We hide our emotions from other people because we don't want them to see how weak we are. We have grown up in a culture that doesn't want to show emotions because society doesn't want to see them. When someone shows his or her emotions, the result is uncertainty, weakness and vulnerability. People don't want to see this in each other, so we all learn to hide our emotions like they're some taboo subject. Now, however, is the time to break out of this emotional prison and share your emotions with others. No, you don't have to share your emotions with the woman standing behind you at the checkout line but it's perfectly normal to share your emotions with the people you trust and love. When you share emotions, the emotional burden you're carrying lessens.

Talk about your emotions. Write about your emotions if you find that easier. Identify the emotions you're feeling and be willing to feel the emotions you're experiencing in your body. Allow yourself to sit with your emotions and be "ok" with the turbulent and challenging ones. The more you sit and care for your emotions, the more their intensity will lessen. As you sit with your emotions, get curious about them. See where in your body you feel them. Examine what these emotions feel like and how heavy they are. See if your emotions have a color, shape, weight or message for you. Get to know your emotions like you're getting to know a stranger.

Once you come out the other side of an emotional storm, be willing to keep your heart open. Every time you face a situation requiring emotional courage or emotional risk, go into your heart. Think of loving thoughts, compassionate feelings or divine blessings to open your heart. Think of your heart as a bubbling stew and you can choose what to toss in there. You can fill it with rocks of judgment, hatred and animosity, or you can toss compassion, love and kindness into the stew. When you confront an emotionally challenging situation, let love and compassion guide you. Think of loving thoughts and open your heart to the challenging situation.

Remember that every situation, every new relationship will make you respond with fear or love. Know that you have a choice in how you respond. If you're regularly processing your emotions and choosing love in all parts of your life, you can respond to new situations with love and openness. You can't live your life in animosity, hatred, jealousy and anger and when it comes to relationships expect your heart to suddenly choose love. The way to be is to choose love in all aspect of your life. It's to take the high road of emotions when you face challenges. Essentially, I'm suggesting you get to choose the emotional being you want to become, but know you must practice the emotional state. You must continually work on raising your emotional state. It doesn't just magically work for your partner and not exist in other parts of your life. Work on your emotional state and being with everyone and become the best person you can be emotionally.

Work on taking risks emotionally. The easiest thing to do is to build a wall around yourself and not let yourself be vulnerable with other people. It's to never share what you're feeling and to hold your emotions close to your heart. You block yourself off from people you care about as you sit behind a fortress of anger and aloofness. You don't let anyone get close because you don't want them to hurt you.

To get stronger emotionally, you must venture out there and take small risks. You don't have to declare your undying love for the next man you meet but you can express yourself to another person when you're still afraid. You can let someone know you're interested in him, you can ask someone out on a date, you can tell someone you admire him. Each of these things takes courage but if you take small steps and practice courage in the face of fear, you will become stronger emotionally.

One last way to bounce back emotionally is to better understand your painful experience and learn from it. More is behind your heartbreak and breakup than that. Whatever was going on in your life at that time has a greater meaning. Can you figure out what it was? Can you give meaning to your pain? Can you understand why it happened and what purpose your past relationship is supposed to serve? When you're a little further away from the pain of heartbreak, you can better understand what happened and why.

If you assign meaning to your pain, you will move forward more easily. If you know why your pain exists, you can move forward more confidently in life. What should you learn about yourself? How did you grow from your experience with your ex? What is this setting you up for in life? If you focus on the empowering reasons why you went through what you did, you can more quickly bounce back emotionally.

Before I go on, I must remind you that these are just some of the many ways to bounce back emotionally. Only you know what works best for you. If you want to reflect on your past and think about the deep emotional pain you've experienced, remind yourself of what you did to bounce back from it. Whatever you did worked. If you had to stop thinking about your emotions or stop your mind from replaying the hurt, do that. If you had to practice silence, do that. If you had to feel your pain deeply and intimately, do that. Think about what has worked for you in the past. Reflect on your own emotional resilience during other challenging times and apply your emotional coping strategies to loving again.

Chapter 5. How do you avoid getting hurt when dating again?

You won't want to date after a heartbreaking relationship. You must find the courage, motivation and inner resilience to get back out there and meet new people. You might not think your heart can withstand any more cracks of pain. It's already in a tattered state so it might not be worth dating at all.

If you are ever going to date or meet new people again and want to make sure you're not going to get hurt, I have some advice. You're better off being single! Relationships come with pain but, as you know, they also create much joy and happiness. Realizing relationships can comprise both pain and joy is encouraging. Also, knowing that the joy far exceeds the pain is encouraging. The pain of past setbacks and failures makes you feel like you're on top of the world when you're in the right relationship. Nothing beats the feeling of being with a compatible and understanding partner – someone who really gets you.

At the same, to be wise in relationships is to know that you can't find all your happiness and joy in your partner. Your companion cannot be your romantic partner, supporter, best friend, priest, therapist, motivator and coach at all times. He'll likely have some bad days too. He'll likely fail and disappoint you (regularly!). To have the healthiest perspective and approach to dating is to make sure you're not putting all your eggs...I mean, hopes and desires...in one person. Instead, think of your potential partner as one part of your life and not your entire existence. You must find fulfillment, joy and happiness outside your partner. Yes, your partner can enhance your life but don't count on him fulfill your happiness at all times.

When we search for partners, we have all kinds of needs we expect from them. This is understandable but is it fair? Should your partner be the one who loves you like no one else can? Is your partner the one who should be there for your emotional healing? Can your partner help erase the pain of your past? As much as we want all this from our partners, wouldn't it be easier to find it within ourselves? Yes, it takes work but this is the healthy way to go about dating. Do your own work. Work on your own healing. Complete yourself. Look for fulfillment, happiness, peace and healing within. Find the tools and professionals to help you do your internal work. When you've found inner happiness and joy, your partner will only enhance it. If you break up, you'll feel less joy, not utter destruction and devastation.

Don't make unrealistic demands of your partner. Don't maintain fairy tale notions of who your ideal partner is or get any funny ideas about him being the perfect man in the relationship. He's likely not going to have all the qualities you desire and may not be everything you're looking for. If you're looking for the perfect man who responds to your every desire, good luck! The Pope is single, George Clooney just got married and Aladdin is a Disney cartoon. Realize that men are people, too! Every person you date is a human being, not a saint. Don't expect them to be saintly super humans who will always do the right things. They won't.

Having expectations of how quickly your relationship should proceed and when you want to get hitched may also lead to more pain. If you're not willing to let the relationship roll on at its own pace, you'll create more confusion and conflict for yourself. You'll be able to tell early on whether the man you're with is serious but getting more specific as to when you want to get engaged and married will create more pain down the road. Let the relationship work on its own timing. You don't have to actively push it towards the place you desire to be. If the guy is not serious, you'll know and can call it quits early.

This brings me to my next point on avoiding pain and disappointment in relationships. Don't overstay relationships which are clearly not working for you. You always know whether the guy is right for you but so often you get sentimental and fearful, thinking you'll never be with someone else, so you put aside the red flags and jump into a relationship you shouldn't be in. You stay in it even if he doesn't treat you well, even if cheats on you or treats you poorly. You know for years that he's the wrong one for you but you continue being idealistic and hopeful. This is a surefire path towards more pain. Get out of a relationship when you know the guy isn't the right one for you. I'll be saying this throughout the book – **you can't be with the right guy if you're with the wrong one**. End bad relationships early to minimize the pain and keep your life open to a suitable partner.

Finally, look at all the men you dated before your ex and even after your ex. Do they share qualities or characteristics with your ex? Can you find common patterns or personality traits? Be aware of the similar unhealthy traits and behaviors of the people you date. Find out what attracts you to them, why that trait draws you in and why it's unhealthy for you to date people like that. If all the people you date are arrogant, chauvinistic and rude, take note of that. If all the men you date are commitment-phobes, take note of that. What are the shared qualities of the people you date and what qualities are unhealthy for you? If you're paying close attention, you can increase your chances of getting out of bad relationships.

Remember, you can't avoid pain in relationships. Getting hurt comes with the territory but, again, how you view hurt matters. If you can focus on the lessons and growth that come from hurt, you can manage the pain the relationship delivers. If you don't learn from them and make the same mistakes without self-awareness, you're stuck in a cycle of pain and heartbreak. Step away from the dating scene, practice some introspection, get some self-understanding and be a smarter dater. Work on finding peace and fulfillment within yourself and you're less likely to let your relationship status affect you.

Chapter 6. How do you trust again?

If a partner has cheated on you or if you didn't initiate the breakup, trusting your ex – and, in the future, any partner – will be hard. You'll likely remember the vows you took, the promises you made and your commitment to each other. If the person you loved most and trusted most broke your trust, how can you ever trust another person? Won't your next partner lie, cheat or walk out of the relationship?

These are all good questions and natural to ask when your relationship ends. Love is fragile and uncertain. It does not travel in a straight line. Here's a situation in which you must loosen your expectations about love and your partner. I'm not saying it's ok if someone violates your trust at will but I am asking you to give your partner a chance. If you can start looking at your partner as an imperfect person doing the best he can, you can see the relationship from a healthier perspective. This perspective is that while we want to have 100-percent trust in each other, things happen. Sometimes our partners fail us because of their shortcomings. Sometimes our partners don't come through for us when they said they would. Maybe your partner didn't do something he promised.

Again, your partner is not perfect and he can break your trust. If you think he IS perfect and should never hurt you in any way, find some good convents to check into. I'm not saying Jesus violates our trust but

God sometimes also lets us down! No one is perfect 100 percent of the time. You can't trust anyone 100 percent of the time. Of course, a betrayal or cheating in your relationship is a clear red flag and indicator of trust. You must take this into account and give weight to it but for smaller violations of trust (like someone cancelling at the last minute or not doing what he said he was going to do), you must be willing to accept that people will sometimes violate your trust. I'm trying to remind you of something you likely already know: people are not perfect. If you believe they are, you are only setting yourself up for heartache.

You know what's stronger than trusting another person? Trusting yourself. Your intuition and inner voice of wisdom are stronger than your trust in any other person. When someone tells you something, makes a promise to you or doesn't come through, trust your intuition to determine whether this person is trustworthy. If you get through your feelings and sentimentality, at a gut level you have an all-knowing inner knowledge. This is a loud and steady voice you likely ignore but this voice is always spot on. If you get quiet and start observing more reflective practices of going within, you will get better at listening to yourself and letting this inner voice guide you.

Listen to this inner voice of wisdom – your intuition – to guide you in relationships. If you trust your inner voice, making decisions about trust becomes easier. What should you consider when you decide how trustworthy a person is? His actions, not his words; make sure what he does measures up to what he says. This doesn't take months or years to figure out. You can come to conclusions and make decisions about trust very early. You can likely make these decisions on your first date. Pay attention to your partner's actions and look out for red flags. See how often he keeps his word and whether he drops the ball on small things or big things. If you are mindful of your partner's actions, notice his trustworthiness and look for serious red flags, you'll know when to call it quits and when to keep going. Be observant, take notes and act when necessary.

You must also create a safe and trusting environment for yourself in the relationship. You must take actions to cultivate trust. If your partner violates your trust, let him know. You can't hold onto grudges and disappointments. You must let him know that he violated your trust and how he did it. Create boundaries for yourself regarding what is acceptable to you and what isn't. If someone crosses the line or hurts you, be willing to do something about it.

Often, when a partner violates the other person's boundaries and trust, that other person looks the other way or ignores the violation because preserving the relationship is more important than any issue! Do not sweep trust issues under the rug for a day that will never come. Be willing to set boundaries for your partner; tell him when he's violated those boundaries and be willing to end the relationship if he violates those boundaries often. Communicate when you feel disappointed and when you feel as though your partner has wronged you. Give him a chance but don't give him unlimited opportunities to violate your trust.

Finally, a caveat or reminder for you about trust and relationships. Just because one serious relationship broke your trust, don't think that all future partners will break your trust. Reflect on your life and think about the relationships in which your partner was trusting and trustworthy. If you can't find examples in your own life, look at the relationships of your friends and family. Affirm to yourself that you can find trustworthy men and be in trust-filled relationships. If you continue to believe that you can't trust another person, you're making life more difficult for yourself. Trust in YOURSELF to make the right decisions about men.

To change your beliefs about trust, look for trust in your everyday relationships. Look for trusting relationships not just with men but with others in your life. Look at past relationships and remind yourself of a partner who was trustworthy. Remind yourself daily through affirmations that trust is possible. Remember, the power to trust is in your hands, not in your partner's.

Chapter 7. How do you
overcome the fear of commitment?

In this chapter, I'm going to address two kinds of commitment. I'll talk about why men are afraid to commit and what you can do about it. Then, I'll ask you to examine your own fears of commitment and share thoughts on how to overcome them.

I can think of three reasons why men don't want to commit in relationships. A man won't commit in a relationship if you're not the right person; he's not going to commit to someone he's not 100 percent sure about. He is also not going to commit if he feels the relationship threatens his freedom or authenticity. If he feels he must become someone he's not, he'll remain a bachelor. Some men are simply not serious about relationships and are not ready to settle down. So, to review: if a man doesn't commit, he might not have found the right person, he might not want to become someone he isn't or he might not be ready to settle down. Other reasons may exist but these three are among the most common.

What can you do as the person in a relationship with a non-committed man? You likely know the patterns and behavior of men who don't commit. Men who don't commit will come on strong and be overly enthusiastic early but will never sacrifice their emotions or time for you. Once you recognize the common traits of non-committed men, you must be on the lookout for this behavior. Once you see this behavior, raise the facts that he's not looking for a committed relationship and you are.

People date for different reasons. Men don't see every relationship as being a long-term one. You must have a conversation and get on the same page that your man is on. If you don't have an understanding early in the relationship, you're only fooling yourself and trying to avoid the unavoidable. If the guy doesn't mention you in his long-term plans, he may not be committed to you for the long run. Your choices with respect to men are to be aware of their tendencies, have a conversation early about what you want and end relationships with those who don't want to commit. Don't blame men for actions you're not willing to tolerate. Don't blame him for being non-committal when you've known this about him for years.

Another major reason why men (and women) don't commit is because they don't want to open themselves up to hurt. Isn't it better to have many superficial relationships that don't mean much than to have one deep, committed one that can last? Isn't it better to keep it cool and casual than to go all in? Isn't it better to be "just friends" or "friends with benefits" than to be partners? You would think so but without the intimacy of a committed partnership, you won't reap the rewards of a deeper connection.

It's natural to want to avoid hurt, especially after you've suffered hurt before. It's natural to want to avoid committing again if you were in a previous long-term relationship or if you were married before but I would say it's not the committed relationship that scares you. What might be scaring you is the potential that the relationship could sour or end. What scares you is the hurt and pain another relationship can cause. So, how do you commit to the real fears of commitment?

To start, you can get to the bottom of your biggest fear. Do a little journaling to understand why you're afraid to commit. Start with this exercise: "I'm afraid to commit because…" and don't stop until you get to the root of this answer. For example, if you write, "I'm afraid to commit because of the pain," keep going, "I'm afraid of the pain because…" Once you acknowledge your fear of something, keep going until you find the root of that fear. When you discover, acknowledge and understand your fear, you will have more clarity. Once you understand your fear, it holds a little less power over you.

I would also argue that a little bit of fear is good. Fear protects you and makes sure you're not making bad decisions. However, fear becomes harmful when it takes over situations entirely and wants all your attention. A smarter way to think about fear is to know it's there for a reason. When you feel fear, remind yourself that while you may be feeling it, excitement might be part of the mix as well. Fear is often an indicator that you're on the right path.

If you're fearful of a relationship, you may have found the "one" and don't want to screw it up. Don't take fear at face value. Something is always going on underneath that fear. You can use fear as an indicator to help you know that a relationship is not right for you. Your fears can be bread crumbs giving you messages for your life's journey. Don't let fear prevent you from seeking love and happiness. Be grateful for the fear and remind yourself that it has a message for you to discover and apply to your life. However, don't give it too much power and don't let it control your life. Depend on fear as an indicator, not as the ruler of your life.

I'm a proponent of small steps in love, career and, essentially, anything in life. You can't commit to giving your life to one person unless you can commit to showing up to a social event. You can't commit to marriage unless you can commit to a date. You can't commit to taking a giant step until you take a baby step. Don't jump off the cliff of commitment. You don't have to believe you're taking a large step towards marriage after your first date. Travel the path towards getting over your fear of commitment one step at a time. Don't let commitment and the responsibility that comes with a committed relationship scare you. Take it one day at a time.

Check in with yourself regularly when you're dating someone and see how you're doing. Does the relationship feel right to you? Are you ready for the next step of commitment? Are you taking the next, most scary, unknown and challenging step? Is it within your comfort level or slightly beyond your comfort level? If you can take small steps and focus on only the most immediate moments of the relationship, you're less likely to let the pain and hurt you've come to associate with a long-term committed relationship terrify you.

Also, consider the worst-case scenario in a committed relationship. What is the absolute worst thing that can happen? This is something I do when I'm taking on any fear in my life. You can use this technique to overcome the fear of commitment too. Think about the worst-case scenario. For example, my divorce was one of the worst things that has ever happened to me. It created the greatest amount of pain and sorrow I've ever experienced. But really, what else did my last relationship bring? It brought out a tremendous amount of self-learning. It forced me to go within and understand myself; it unleashed the greatest amount of growth in my life.

My breakup also helped me clarify who I am. It helped me start living a more authentic life and unleashed the power of my creative dreams. I say all of this simply to remind you that even if you have a long-term committed marriage or relationship that ends, you can get through it. You can receive many gifts and rewards from having survived a difficult relationship. As your parents and best friends remind you, it's not the end of the world. Remind yourself that good – a lot of good and wisdom – can come from heartbreak. Even if you go all in, get hurt and have a heart-shattering experience, you will advance in your growth, become smarter in relationships and be more ready for your next relationship.

Yes, ends come with pain and suffering but if a relationship works, you're on the path to love and fulfillment.

Chapter 8. How do you deal with anxiety and fear of loving again?

Similar to the fear of commitment, you can simply be fearful of getting out there and meeting people again. You could fear dating, romance or any relationship. How do you get over this fear of love in general?

Let's use the small-step strategy I spoke about in the previous chapter. You wouldn't get right back out there and start dating again. Why not start small? Why not start enjoying your life, getting social and meeting people in general? It took me a long time to get to the point where I wanted to meet people again. That's because in my mind I thought all introductions would be about dating. But they weren't. I've met many good friends who are working on various spiritual practices and creative arts, who are pursuing their dreams. Many kind, generous, funny and caring people are in the world. You don't have to date them all or have breath-taking, earth-shaking romances with all of them. You can simply be friends and get to know people for the sake of friendship, kindness and caring.

In fact, use friendships and social events to reduce your fear of people in general. So you don't feel too far out of your comfort zone, look for events and activities you already enjoy. Attend events at which you'll have mutual interests with the people already there or at which you'll know quite a few of the people. Having common friends or common interests in group settings will help you more easily meet and mingle with new people. Be as comfortable as possible when you're in larger groups; this will help reduce the anxiety of being in a room of strangers. Meeting new people will also help reduce your fears of meeting potential partners. Again, the intention at the beginning isn't to meet a new partner. It's simply to get out there and meet new people while being comfortable with the process.

Another thing to work on is your belief system regarding love. You have likely filled your mind, heart and body with strong feelings about love and relationships. Many of these sentiments and thoughts about relationships are likely negative. If we were conversing now and I asked you what you thought about relationships, you could likely give me a laundry list of negative and fear-based thoughts. It might help for you to speak these thoughts, be aware of them or write them down. Once you clarify all your negative vibes on relationships, start challenging each one. Write down a negative belief and then write down why it's not true. Write down alternatives to the thought. Examples are below:

Belief: I don't believe I will ever be in a relationship. I am not made for relationships.

Why it's false: You were in a relationship before. People have expressed interest in you and you have wanted to be in relationships.

Alternative: You can be in a relationship if you do some inner work on yourself. Changing your beliefs and taking on your fears can help you be in a relationship. Shifting your perspective and belief system can help you welcome love.

Belief: I don't believe I'm worthy or good enough for the men I admire.

Why it's false: This stems entirely from your perception and inner belief. You have been good enough for friendships, relationships and connections with family. Lots of people consider you worthy and good enough.

Alternative: You are worthy and enough. You may not believe it because of life's happenings but deep within, you know you are enough just the way you are. Your self-acceptance and belief in yourself are the critical steps to any relationship. You don't need others to find you worthy. You just have to find yourself worthy and accept yourself.

Understand and pinpoint your false and unhealthy beliefs about yourself. Come up with a long list of reasons why your beliefs aren't true and what alternatives exist. You can take a few minutes to do this now or every day. The next step is to look for positive beliefs and validation that supports those beliefs.

If you want to shift your belief about worthiness, think about everything in your life that has helped you feel worthy. Affirm to yourself that you are worthy and back up your affirmation every day with thoughts of your worthiness. Support your new belief with facts you might have ignored in the past. You are worthy because your parents loved you unconditionally and told you so your entire life. You are worthy because your kids love you and accept you completely. You are worthy because you are part of the divine, universal fabric. You are worthy as a person who believes in compassion, kindness and love. You are worthy because you give regularly, help abundantly and try to make the world a better place everywhere you go.

Yes, you're essentially becoming your own cheerleader and reminding your belief system every day that it has things wrong. You are reminding yourself of why you are worthy, why you deserve love, why you're smart about love or why you're enough just the way you are. Someone else won't find you worthy and lovable if you don't do the same yourself. If your limitations are in your belief system and thoughts, wouldn't it make sense to do the work within? Wouldn't it make sense to work on those beliefs within your control? You can't influence romance or meeting new people but you can shift your internal thoughts and beliefs about romance. If you're holding onto negative and disempowering views of relationships, here's how to work on those.

Become aware of those beliefs and views. Take the power away from them and substitute new thoughts and beliefs for the older ones that don't serve you well. Do this daily and often so you can work on your belief system regularly. If you don't believe you're worthy and deserving of a relationship, you've already lost the mental battle. At this point, it has nothing to do with partners and relationships. It involves only your relationship with yourself. If you don't believe you're worthy or enough for a relationship, you must do nothing more than change those beliefs. If you don't believe you will ever be in a relationship, your most important work is to understand and change that belief.

You're not a computer, but if you were, you could not enter information contrary to what you expected in the output. If this were a math problem, you couldn't put the wrong variable on one side of the equation and expect to get the right answer. What I'm saying is you can't hold onto contrary and negative internal beliefs and expect your external world to give you something different. For example, if you believe the world is evil and going to hell, what types of daily circumstances are you more likely to notice? If you believe the world is kind and abundant, what types of events will you notice? The same applies to your life.

One last way I would suggest dealing with fear is living in the present moment. I know this is a very Zen-like thing to say but here's what I mean. Your fear exists only in your past and future. You are fearful because you're thinking about what happened in your past and you're worried about what's going to happen in the future. You are fearful of your past because you believe your previous relationships will show up in your next relationship. You are fearful of your future because of your uncertainty and belief that the future will be a repeat of what happened before. If you hold these beliefs and fears, complete the exercise I just shared with you about shifting your beliefs. You can figure out for yourself why your fears are unfounded and replace them with more empowering beliefs.

As far as why living in the moment helps, I want to show you that, in this present moment, no fears exist. If you capture a second or a minute or a moment of time and examine it, you will see no fears right now. Close your eyes for ten seconds and breathe. Did you notice any fear? Do you have anything to be scared about? In this very second, you can't come up with fears of the past or future. All you have in this moment is this moment. That's it. Nothing to fear. So instead of hibernating in the past or getting anxious about the future, bring yourself to this moment and live in this place more than in the other places.

I have found that, to live in the present moment, mindfulness and meditative practices help. I can't go into detail here because this isn't a present-moment-living book but I want to at least share what worked for me in case you are looking for practices that will allow you to live in the moment more. (If you need a book on this, I recommend Jon

Kabat-Zinn's **Wherever You Go, There You Are**.) For example, when I meditate daily I focus on my breath the entire time. This allows me to be present with my breath. Also, when I take a walk or write, I am fully present with this activity. I don't let thoughts of the past or the future pull me away from what I'm doing at the moment. Concentrate on your daily activities so you're focusing on the task at hand.

When you're focusing on the now, you're less likely to revisit the pain of the past or ponder the uncertainty of the future. I've read about and applied this kind of concentration to daily tasks and chores. It works! If you're washing dishes, cleaning the yard or driving, fully immerse yourself in the activity. During this time, don't allow yourself to travel away to another time. In some ways, reading books or watching movies does the same thing but I feel like these activities are distractions away from the present moment, not a means of focusing on the present moment.

If you can focus your mind on right now, you will not let fear influence you as much. You won't let the past or the future pull you away as easily. You won't live each day thinking about how much pain you endured in your previous relationships and why you'll see that pain again in your future relationships. Remember, in this moment no fear exists. In love, relationships and life, focus on the moment right in front of you.

Chapter 9. How do you deal with rejection?

Each rejection after my divorce felt like a new heartbreak. I'm talking about rejection that comes when someone is not interested in you, when someone doesn't call you back or doesn't respond with the same feelings you have for them. When you start caring about someone new and he doesn't care about you, your heart breaks again. You begin to believe that all men are the same and that love isn't in the stars for you!

Rejection can be excruciatingly painful after a breakup or divorce. You have already suffered rejection in a significant way, especially if you were the person who didn't want the breakup. When your ex broke up with you, you experienced pain but each new rejection, when you're trying to get out of there, can seem even more painful.

When I was fresh out of the divorce, a rejection from a woman was the worst feeling to experience. I later realized that I hadn't gotten over the divorce yet, so it was only natural that I would feel a greater sense of rejection. If you're feeling bad about rejection, check in with a couple of things. First, make sure you've done the necessary work to heal from the past and let go of the pain your ex caused. You cannot bounce back or move forward romantically until you've processed the hurt and let go of your ex. If you don't do it now, your pain and hurt will surface later in another relationship. Don't start dating seriously simply to bounce back from your ex or because you believe it is the best way to move on. Often, the best way to move on is to grieve, heal and let go of the past before you get into a new relationship.

The second thing you should consider when you're facing rejection is whether you fully accept and love yourself. If your ex and others rejected you and you're facing rejection in an unusually harsh way, see if you've fallen into the habit of rejecting yourself. Do you put yourself down, devalue yourself and think you're not good enough? These may be subconscious beliefs you must deal with. You must be willing to do the work to love and accept yourself first.

You can take actions to show yourself love and cultivate love for yourself from within. You can also write out your beliefs about yourself and examine what you believe about yourself. You can cultivate compassion and kindness for yourself. This is similar to cultivating love. Within yourself, you feel the feelings of compassion you have for people you love or causes you care about. Those feelings are like a candle burning brightly, and you shine that candle on yourself. You feel the light of compassion within you and you let that compassion shine on you when you're saying bad things about yourself, when you feel bad about yourself or when you're mentally rejecting yourself. You give yourself the same light of compassion you would give to others in your life who are struggling or sabotaging themselves.

Try to get to the bottom of the rejection. See where these feelings of rejection come from. If you can pinpoint the moment when you suffered your initial rejection, when you felt the pangs of rejection most and whose rejection hurt you the most, it can help. You likely experienced rejection early in your life and by people who were supposed to have loved you. Or you experienced heartbreak and pain in your youth. These feelings don't go away and continue finding triggers throughout our life. Try to understand what your source of rejection is and what's behind it. If you know the source and what triggers rejection, you can welcome rejection much more easily into your life. You can welcome it in like an old friend or a nemesis you've had a relationship with instead of a combative stranger who is dueling you to the death!

Like visiting the dentist and falling off a bicycle when you're learning to ride, rejection gets easier with experience. You likely rejections experiences in your work life if you have ever tried to sell something or persuade someone.

Throughout my life in the U.S., I've had a passion for grassroots politics. Grassroots politics is when you talk to actual people – your regular, everyday American – to encourage them to support an issue or candidate you are championing. I've volunteered for political campaigns and worked for candidates by asking voters to support the person I was supporting. I've done this through both phone and face-to-face contact. I've met voters at community events, their apartments or their homes to speak to them directly and ask for their vote.

What does this have to do with rejection and love? Well, when I talk to people, many of them reject me. Usually a third of the people I talk to are supportive, a third are not and a third are undecided. It's the third who are non-supportive who I want to talk about because they've taught me most of what I know about rejection. Some have had harsh words for me; some have shut the door in my face, while some have simply hung up the phone. People have varied reactions when they confront a choice or candidate they don't support.

Somehow in these situations, I learned not to take rejection personally. I've learned that my candidate is not the right person for everyone. I've learned I can encounter rejection at one door and find myself in front of a voter who loves my candidate at the next. I've learned I can face rejected once but if I keep going long enough, I'll find people who thank me and encourage me to keep going. I've learned that how people react has more to do with them than with me. I've learned that I must get back out there and fight for votes. If I lose one vote at one house, it's not the end of the game. I take the bigger, long-distance view and keep going. For every person who hates my candidate, another one loves my candidate.

I think when the door has slammed enough in your face during a campaign or a sales call, or when you make requests of other people, you gain deep insight into dealing with rejection in romance. (I wonder what I'd name that book if I wrote it – *The Business of Love* (or *Sales Strategies for Your Love Life*.) You learn that after enough rejection, you'll find people who like your politics and want to support you. You learn that people's reactions have little to do with you but instead are about their preferences and choices. You learn that you can persuade and convince some people if you make good arguments. You learn that someone who doesn't like your candidate one day can learn to like your candidate over time. You learn to keep going when you feel discouraged or tired because the next positive reaction or supporter may be at the next house.

The situation is the same with romantic relationships but usually you want to give up rather than try again. This usually happens after one or two rejections, not hundreds. You base your opinion on one or two people, not dozens. If five people reject you, or 10, you start believing that everyone doesn't like you or will reject you. It usually doesn't take five or 10 people; sometimes just one person rejecting you is enough to feel terrible about yourself, as though the opposite sex doesn't want you. Doesn't this seem strange – to allow a small number of rejections to determine our desirability?

A healthier way to think about rejections – and the mindset I used when working in politics – is that you must encounter enough rejections to get yourself closer to the right people or person. If you get enough rejections, you're trying. You're putting yourself out there and taking risks with each new person. Each rejection moves you closer to the person you should be with. Each rejection is a reminder of who would be a better fit for you. Each rejection is a reminder of who you should avoid. Instead of seeing rejection as a dead end or a failure, why not see it from a perspective of possibility and hope? Finding the wrong person helps you move closer to the right person.

The person who rejected you could have done so for many reasons. He could have other things going on in his life. He may not have healed from a past relationship. He could be a commitment-phobe. He could be uninterested for many reasons, not simply because he's not attracted to you. Again, if his rejection is because he's not attracted to you, he might simply have a personal preference. One person's personal preference. Just because one person doesn't appreciate you doesn't mean no one is interested in you.

Also, consider this: What if the person rejecting you is, in fact, rejecting himself? When others say "no" to you or say they are "not interested" in you, they are rejecting themselves from you. Aren't they ultimately doing you a favor? You could end up in a wrong or dysfunctional relationship but instead the person rejecting you is giving you a way out and saving you years of heartache.

You can let rejection crush you or you can regard it as a badge of honor. You can see rejection as a way of reaching your right partner. You can see that the more you experience rejection, the closer you get to the person who is right for you. You can see surviving rejection as a mark of resilience, as indicative of someone who doesn't give up. You can see rejection as the price you pay for joy and happiness. Romantic rejections will give you the grit you need to deal with any rejection that comes up in your life. As with other rejections, you're not going to let one person's opinions paralyze you. You're going to get up and keep going. You're going to keep going, keep searching and keep taking risks until you find the right person.

The better you deal with rejection in romance, the better you deal with rejection in all aspects of your life. The more you face rejection, the better you get at dealing with it. Also, the more you face rejection, the less you feel the sting of one rejection. Yes! The secret isn't to catch yourself up in one rejection but to turn it into a game, to go out there and welcome more rejection into your life. Once you realize you can deal with many rejections, you'll see things falling into place. Romance will be in the mix. Rejection is the small price we pay to get the lives we want.

Remember that although people can reject their interest in you, no one can really reject you if you refuse to reject yourself. This goes back to self-worth and worthiness, which we talked about earlier. If you're enough, no one else should make you feel less than enough. In your deepest and worthiest place, where you're full of light and spirit, you are complete and enough by yourself. In a spiritual realm, you are part of the greater universe and you are complete in that place. No person, no opinion, no relationship can change that about you. If you step into your worthiness and fully and completely accept yourself for who you are, you won't let any other person determine your desirability or worth.

Chapter 10. When should you start dating again?

Do not jump back into romance after a breakup from a long-term relationship. Everyone advises you not to jump into a new relationship but you're ready to find the next available single man who crosses your path. Even if he's semi-single or in the process of getting divorced, don't fall for it. The man of your dreams is NOT waiting for you at the exit sign of your last relationship.

You have no reason to rush into another relationship. You also have no reason to fall into a deep depression, believe you're unworthy and vow to never love again. A balance exists. I have some suggestions of things you can reflect upon, uncover and discover for yourself before you start dating.

One big thing to figure out before you start dating again is what you need to learn about yourself after this breakup. Very likely it's not the breakup or divorce that is your sole problem. From my own experience and from the people I've spoken to, I've found there are deeper unresolved issues or completely unrelated issues percolating beneath the surface of heartbreak.

Your job is to figure this out. It may require reflection, introspection, therapy and self-understanding. I would say the end of the relationship was at a very superficial level; instead, what was going on underneath the relationship? What was coming up from your past? What unresolved issues are you dealing with? What characteristics or personality traits do you need to work on? What other aspects of your life are in turmoil? What childhood memory are you not able to forget? This is the job at hand. You can start journaling these questions or simply acknowledge the answers you already know. What has been bothering you?

Once you figure this out and get to the bottom of the emotional, mental, work-related or childhood-related issue, you will have the awareness and foresight to move on. You can't fix what you don't know. Yes, someone may have wheeled you into the hospital because of the heart attack but I'm asking you to get into which lifestyle choices and past decisions created the conditions for the heart attack? The problem is the superficial. We need you to figure out what's lying under the problem. What is the inner work you need to do?

It would be better if you waited to date until you have experienced some healing or are actively working on the wounds. Therapy is one way to do this but your own personal growth plan for healing will suffice. Once you figure out your internal issues, you (alone or with the help of a professional) must come up with solutions to grow, heal the wounds within or bounce back from whatever it is that's keeping you stuck. What will you need to move forward? What is holding you back internally? How will you work on these struggles each and every day? Sometimes awareness is all you need. Acceptance and understanding of your wounds is always a good start.

What did your relationship teach you about your ex, yourself and your relationship together? Do not pass go or collect $200 until you figure this out. Profound lessons were waiting for you in heartbreak. You're not doing yourself any favors if you don't look at the lessons your relationship can teach you. Did you learn you were dealing with insecurities and low self-esteem? Did you learn you don't have the healthy skills to be in a relationship? Did you learn you never discovered how to express love to another person or have healthy conflicts with your lover? Did you learn you didn't know how to communicate well? Whatever it is you discovered in love, you must notice, examine and study it. Your past is your teacher for your future.

In addition to working on yourself, the post-breakup period is a good time to reflect upon the kind of person you want in your life. This is one of the benefits of Indian arranged marriages in my culture. I did not go through this process but that's a story for another day. Even before making introductions, families do copious amounts of work to find the ideal mate for their son or daughter. Families look for common factors in both sides. They look for social compatibility, cultural compatibility, religious compatibility and, yes, maybe even professional compatibility. Before families introduce their kids to each other, they research many of these factors, snooping around and pursuing information like the CIA on a mission. Often, the matches work well because couples find that they have much in common and come from similar backgrounds.

How can you use these strategies in the Western world? Figure out who exactly you want in your life. Think about your world perspective, your values and your beliefs. Be aware of the qualities and the person you want in your life. Do some visualizing and use this worksheet I created for my blog. Before you start dating, note the characteristics, qualities and interests you want in your future partner. We plan so much of our lives, like college and our careers. Should we spend a little bit of time planning for our partners? Once you complete this exercise, you'll obtain more clarity about where you can find a partner like this.

Don't swim in the waters of rebound dating. Take this well-deserved time to complete the work on yourself. Figure out what lessons you need to learn and reflect on the discoveries you've made about yourself. Do the work to grow, heal and understand yourself from the past relationship. Only once you've done that should you start developing ideas about the right person for you. Fill out the worksheet I've included to gain clarity and visualize your next compatible match. Once you've done these things, enter the dating world as a wiser, smarter and more confident person.

Enter the dating world with a relaxed and stress-free attitude, not when you're carrying the burdens and pains of the past. Go back in with a casual and playful nature. Don't maintain heavy expectations, pressures or strict timelines. This is romance, after all, not something completely in your hands. A bit of magic and uncertainty exist in dating and relationships – a light-heartedness, kindness and chemistry you can't plan for or predict. So, yes, take the process seriously but not too seriously that you overlook the unexpected match or the soulmate sitting next to you on the train.

Chapter 11. Where do you meet people?

One of the biggest challenges you'll encounter when you start dating again is figuring out where to meet other single people. I've found that the most ineffective way to date is online! I don't feel as though the online world is real. I know, I know, plenty of people have met their partners and life-long loves online. It just doesn't seem to work for me. Well, let me rephrase that. It's not that you can't meet online through various activities and shared interests. I'm just not a fan of online dating, specifically, visiting dating websites to search for romantic partners. For me, online dating is out but meeting people online on non-dating websites seems to work.

An interesting source of potential leads – and I know this is not going to help most of you reading this book – is through blogging. Don't worry, I'll expand on this to reveal what seems to work for me. It's not blogging or being online per se that has led to my meeting new people; rather, it is the fact that I am at a place where I do what I enjoy. Blogging takes place in a group setting and is a public forum containing people with similar interests. So, while I can't recommend going out and starting a blog solely to meet potential partners, I can recommend a few broader ideas.

What groups, online and offline, share your interests? Do you enjoy a particular game or genre of movies or books? Do you have a unique interest, like coffee or restaurants? Whatever you are most passionate about, look for groups of interested people who are already doing those things online and start participating in those communities. Ask questions, answer questions and be helpful. In the online world, you never know who you will meet who is similar to you and who has shared interests.

I would say the same thing about the offline "real world." Find groups that share your interests and participate in their activities. Visit places where you are likely to find like-minded individuals and immerse yourself in those activities. You can even be a little strategic about it and consider the places where you might find people like you.

My own self-knowledge tells me I am drawn to areas with creative or spiritual people. I am drawn to workshops about writing, blogging, finding inter-faith connections and improving oneself spiritually. I know the woman I'm looking for values spirit, growth and self-improvement, so I immerse myself in that circle.

What circle is your future partner a part of? What do you enjoy doing? What topics are you drawn to when you go to the bookstore? Whatever it is you enjoy doing or are passionate about, get involved in local groups and communities that focus on the same things. Go for your interest and passion and you will find people who share those with you. Don't go specifically to meet people of the opposite sex. Who knows – maybe you'll make friends, meet your best friend or find activity partners who are into the same things you are. Focus on finding people with similar interests, doing activities you enjoy and meeting new people.

Not only should you engage in group activities you enjoy and in a group setting, you should meet up with people you enjoy spending time with. Here's what I've come to learn about people who are compatible with you. It's only logical, if you think about it. Your potential partner – and someone you would be interested in – is likely very similar to your close circle of friends. You picked your friends because they have values, worldviews and interests like yours. These are the people you choose to spend time with. Likely, your group of closest friends contains people you look up to and admire. If these are people you're already in sync with and are good matches for you, doesn't it make sense that their friends will also be very similar to you? Your friends' friends will make for great friendship – and possibly dating – material, so spend time with them. Say "yes" to dinner invites and parties your friends host. Very likely, the people you're interested in already know the people you are friends with.

A few more ideas of places where you can find people who might be interested in you: Volunteer or charity events and fundraisers are good places to meet people. So are social events surrounding causes or community events relating to shared goals. Work dinners and networking events that relate to your work life. Gyms, community centers and shared workout facilities, including yoga studios and pools. See who works in different offices around your company. Look for neighbors who live in your vicinity. Let your friends and family be on the lookout as well. Let them know you're open to meeting new people and ask them to check in with their own networks of people.

You never know where you'll meet the partner of your dreams. More than likely, he is very close to you. He is only one event, one connection or one or two houses away. I don't believe we must travel throughout the world to find the love of our lives. I have a strong feeling that the person you're looking for is looking for you too. All you have to do is take a risk, venture out and pay attention to the people in your inner circle (and the people they know).

One last note is to remind you to stay away from the old stomping grounds where you met your ex. Avoid the circles and places where you hung out when you started dating him. Also, avoid hook-up joints, clubs, bars and other "traditional" dating places that are likely to net low-quality men. Don't make the same mistakes and wonder why you can't find a good man. Knowing where NOT to meet people is just as important as knowing where to meet people.

Chapter 12. How do you find an emotionally available partner?

Before you look for an emotionally available partner, check in with yourself. How are you doing in the emotion department? Have you moved on from your past? Are you comfortable dealing with intimacy? Are you willing to talk about your emotions and your vulnerabilities? You may think you're emotionally available but you never know until you do your own work. See if you're able to speak with others openly, share your feelings honestly and experience pain.

If you feel you are emotionally available, you can find a similarly emotionally available partner by being attentive. Once you work on your own issues with emotional strength and openness, notice how your potential partner handles his emotions. Take notes and observe how your partner responds, reacts and manages his emotional well-being with you and everyone else in his life. You can learn a lot by your emotional responses to his family, friends and inner circle. If he acts in an unhealthy or toxic way towards the people he loves, that's a big red flag.

Let your partner know what you're looking for emotionally. If it's not working for you, let your partner know what you need from him. Communicate instead of hiding your emotional needs. Instruct him if necessary. Show him what you need from him. Ask for what you need.

Don't bottle up your emotional needs or believe your partner will understand what you want without your saying it. Speak out your needs and communicate. Your partner cannot predict, guess or use telepathy to understand what you need from him.

If you've communicated your needs but he doesn't show up or make improvements in the way he shows up emotionally, you have a choice. You can decide he's doing the best he can and will get there someday or you can decide, no, you've had enough. If you see improvements after you inform him of your needs, hope exists. If you see the same patterns over and over, you're stuck in the wrong relationship. At some point, you must decide whether this is a cause worth staying for or if it's a lost cause. If he shows no improvement or doesn't even attempt to meet you emotionally, it's time to move on.

The way to find an emotionally available partner is to make sure you're emotionally available for a relationship yourself. When you have a new partner, see how he handles himself emotionally with both you and others in his life. You will know from your first several conversations whether he can be open emotionally.

Learn to be more aware of the signs of emotional availability. Determine for yourself what emotional availability looks like and be aware of it when you are dating. An emotionally available partner will share his feelings for you and be willing to listen to your feelings. An emotionally available partner will be there for you with compassion and empathy. He will offer supportive words and a listening ear. An available partner will allow you to share your secrets and vulnerabilities without judging you or putting you down. An emotionally available partner will make time and space for you.

Of course, men are never the best at all these things and they will not be as emotionally expressive as you want them to be but a clear distinction exists. Some men will hide their feelings at all costs and never let you into their emotional space, while others may do so occasionally. A very few may be very emotionally expressive and understanding. If he grew up in an emotionally healthy family, for example, he may be well-versed in the language of emotions. Your job, again, is to know what emotional availability looks like, be aware of it and be willing to act on it once you know whether someone is right (or not right) for you.

If he has the potential to be there for you emotionally, keep working on the relationship. If not, end the relationship and move on with your life. The quicker you make this decision, the easier it will be to find the partner who's right for you.

Most of the time you won't learn until later whether a partner is emotionally open. Even if he's not the person you want emotionally, you never bring up this issue or you assume things will get better later. You think he's not opening up to you because he doesn't know you well enough yet. We use a myriad of excuses to put up with people who are incompatible with us. You might put up with the worst kind of behavior and people because you don't want to suffer heartbreak and loneliness. You would rather have an emotionally unavailable partner than no partner at all.

What I'm asking you to do is choose the person who's right for you and let go of people who are not. You will find emotionally available partners by screening them and then letting them into your life. You will find emotionally available partners by letting go of the emotionally unavailable ones. You will find emotionally healthy partners by ending relationships with those who are not.

Chapter 13. How do you choose the right partner?

You keep getting stuck in the same unhealthy relationships. You fall in love with the wrong people: the distant, the emotionally unavailable, the people who betray you and who don't stay. After each bad relationship, you wonder, *'What went wrong?'* You wonder what's preventing you from choosing and keeping the right partner.

To choose the right partner, you must clarify who you're looking for. We often seek partners the way we go about shopping. You walk into a store and see what's available. You keep walking through the store until you find something that catches your eye. You try it on, you like it and you buy it.

Unless, of course, you're buying something you are going to spend a lot of money on, like a house or a car. In that situation, you do a lot of planning and research to figure out exactly what house or car you want based on your needs and desires. Isn't it interesting that for something invaluable we roam the stores while for something valuable we plan ahead? When dating, shop for a partner as though you're shopping for a life-changing, expensive item! Do your research, plan ahead, know what you're looking for.

Get clear on who you want. Understand yourself enough to know what type of person is a good fit for you. This takes work on your part. You don't have to settle for any man. You don't have to go blindly into the dating field without any idea of what kind of partner you want. Your work is realizing who you are and what you want. It's asking yourself what qualities are essential to you. It's asking yourself what you'll tolerate and what you won't. It's setting healthy boundaries for yourself so no man will cross or trample on them.

Stay diligent in finding a partner who fits this profile – though make sure the profile is reasonable, of course. If you're looking for someone with a great dental practice, a great body, a great smile, and a caring and generous personality, someone who will love you and your kids, good luck! I'm not saying all-around men are rare; instead, I'm saying that having the highest of expectations will reduce your number of potential matches. While you should have a good idea of who you're looking for, don't use an automatic litmus test to eliminate potential partners if a man doesn't have a certain personality or look a certain way. He might be extremely compatible with you. You just have to get past breaking the ice to see how compatible he actually is.

When choosing partners, go for substance over superficiality. Choose character over charm. I know you want to be physically attracted to a person. You want a good-looking partner. Who doesn't? But I also know you can't see a person's heart, soul and character until you get to know him.

Instead of focusing on what your ideal partner looks like, how tall he is and how much he weighs, focus on getting to know a person for who he is. The goal isn't to find a partner who will look good in your wedding photos but to find a partner who is compatible with you and who will be there for you in the long run. Instead of looks or clothing, seek a partner who has staying power. Look for compassion, kindness and a similar sensibility. Look for a partner who shares your worldview and who has similar values.

The best way to choose the right partner is to choose yourself first. Huh? You might be scratching your head. I'm asking you to choose yourself so you'll find the joy within. I talk about this in much more detail in Chapter 15, where I encourage you to become the best version of yourself, find your own happiness and start living your best life. I suggest that you get comfortable with yourself and choose yourself because this will be the best space to meet a partner. It's about coming from and living in a place of worthiness and happiness. The better you're doing in life, the better the partner coming into your life will be.

Make it your priority to find love, joy and happiness within. Don't make your life's priority finding a partner who can make you happy. No one can make you happy but yourself. No one can complete you but you. You may want someone to love you like no one has loved you before. I know the feeling. I desperately wanted that too but I've learned those types of relationships aren't healthy and can lead to much greater heartbreak. If you depend on your partner's affection for a sense of love and belonging, know that it can leave you at any time.

Don't let someone else's love be your light. Cultivate the light within so another person's love won't manipulate you or hold you captive. Use someone else's light to shine brighter yourself.

You choose the right partner by allowing your partner's behavior and commitment be a guide. So often we find ourselves in messed-up relationships with people who are not good for us. You know many of these relationships should have ended a long time ago but you refuse to end them. From day one you've known about many of his characteristics yet you ignore your instincts, overlook his behavior and trust he will improve.

When you have idealistic notions about someone becoming what he's not, you're being delusional. Hold your partner accountable for his actions and behavior. Use patterns of unhealthy behavior to decide what you'll do with the relationship. Accept your partner for where he is in life, not where you want to see him in five years. Believe him when he shows you who he is. Decide to be with him or not be with him according to who he is today, not who he might be years from now.

To create a picture of your man and determine whether he's right for you, let your intuition guide the way. Don't let your hormones or feelings for him lead you; instead, rely on the soft-spoken inner voice of knowing. You have a wise guide and guardian angel who speaks to you via your intuition. It's simply knowing in your stomach and your heart whether he's the right one for you.

Chapter 14. How do you know you've found the right person?

Let's say you've been dating for a while and you've met someone who seems to fit all the criteria you've been looking for. How do you know this is the person for you? How do you know this is the long-term, steady partner you've been looking for? How do you know whether you should keep him or dump him?

If you've been doing some of the exercises and suggestions in this book, you will know whether the person you've found fits all the criteria you're looking for. In previous chapters, I provided tools for clarifying your potential partner. If you've done this work and the person you've visualized – or the person who has the qualities you desire – shows up, you're on the right path.

You have likely found your partner because he sees the world the way you do and has the same values you do. A shared perspective, shared political outlook and shared religious background are all things to look for in a partner. I'm not suggesting you must practice the same religion or have the same political beliefs but I think underlying your politics and religion are core values you should look for in a partner. A shared purpose with respect to why you're both here or a shared meaning for your existence also boost compatibility.

I don't think I can overstress the importance of your intuition in knowing who is right for you. If you listen to this inner voice, you'll know whether the person you're with is the right person. Often, we know this in advance but we ignore this voice. We have so much going on and we become distracted, so we don't stop to listen. If you're not sure about someone, get quiet and go within. Check in with your intuition and ask it if the person you're with is right for you. This deep inner-knowing is more powerful than any other sign you could receive or opinion you could get from any friend. You don't have to ask anyone you know about whether he's the right one. You know and that's all that matters. If he's not the right one, your job is to end the relationship and move on.

There are other qualities in a partner you should check on to see if he is right for you. Does your partner make you feel safe? Can you fight and argue in a safe, non-threatening way? Can you disagree without feeling like the relationship is going to end? Can you have healthy discussions during which both of you talk about what's bothering you? Can you be in a safe space in your relationship and not threaten or blackmail each other when you disagree? You want to be sure the person you're with can handle the situation when things get heated. Everyone can be there for the good parts of a relationship. Is your guy capable of handling the messy and challenging parts?

When you have disagreements or heated arguments, you want a partner who can bounce back. How good are you together in repairing and healing a wound in the relationship? How well do you both work through issues? Can you both forgive each other, make space for each other and move on after you've argued? Can you let go of grudges after fights? Can you get back on the same page after you've fought? Will you both learn from your mistakes and not repeat the pattern of fighting? Make sure you are with a partner you can grow and improve with over time. A partner who will learn from his mistakes and make sure you don't end up in the same place over and over. Less ego and more humility are important qualities of healthy relationships.

Another way to know you've found the right person is that you accept each other without trying to change each other. Are you willing to accept him for who he is and will he accept you for who you are? Do you say things like, "I wish you were more like this…" or "I want you to be more this kind of person…" If you're saying these kinds of things, you're likely not accepting the person for who they are today.

I've never found people to change in relationships. Well, at least I've never found partners who change based on the other partner's demands. I've found partners who change when they trust their partner. I've found people change when the relationship contains compassion and acceptance. When you love and accept a person for where he is in life, he will naturally strive to make changes and become the version of himself you like. However, pressuring a partner or wishing he were someone he's not can only damage the relationship.

You also know you are with the right person when you've seen him at his best and his worst. If you have seen his worst and you can deal with those behaviors and tendencies (and, again, if the situation feels safe to you), you're on the right track. If at his worst the person has violent blow-ups and threatens to stab you, the relationship will not work. Be mindful of the person's worst moments and make sure you take them into account when you're deciding whether to stay and work on the relationship.

Also, determine whether how he shows up in the relationship for you is the same way he shows up for other people. If he's good to you and bad to his family, you've found a red flag. If he's bad to you and good to his friends, you've found a different red flag. You want a partner who is consistent and who treats everyone with respect. You want someone who is authentic in all his relationships, not putting on a show for you or any of the people in his life.

Finally, you want someone who doesn't see the relationship as an end all and be all. Being in a relationship is good but it isn't the end. I would say that being in a relationship is like getting into the same boat; in no way does admission mean you'll be happy or get to your desired destination. You want to make sure you're not with a pirate or someone who will throw you overboard. You want to make sure you're with someone who understands that the journey starts when you're in a relationship. You must find someone who is willing to work on the relationship once they are in one.

I will continue repeating this: You cannot be with the right person if you're with the wrong one. If upon further reflection you're sure he's not the one and he's not healthy for you, your world and life are not over. When you let go of the wrong person in your life, you make room for the right one. Do not let an unhealthy partner overstay his welcome. Be grateful you met him and for the positive impact on your life but let him go if he doesn't belong there. Most of the time the relationship won't get better; it will only get worse.

Chapter 15. What can you do to find your ideal partner?

Much of this book has been about finding your ideal partner. To find your ideal partner, you must be your ideal and highest self. That's what this chapter is about. I want to talk about all the ways you can become the best version of yourself so you can welcome your ideal partner into your life.

One important thing you can do for your love life – and your life in general – is focus on what you do have. When people are trying to date, they often find themselves caught up in their personal faults and everything their lives lack. Don't date from a place of lack; focus on what you do have. Focus on what's going well for you. Reaffirm your qualities, characteristics and positive attributes. Think about how lucky a partner would be to have someone like you. Also, reflect on all the areas of your life that are going well. A small gratitude practice for all the things working in your life would be helpful. If relationships with your family are good, if you like your job, if you're living where you want to live, be grateful for all those things.

When you're in a place of gratitude, you're more open and welcoming. You're in a higher place in terms of energy. When you're not wrapped up in a "woe is me" attitude, you're likely to invite in higher-caliber and higher-energy individuals. You are less likely to run into people who are also focusing on lack. Instead, you will encounter people coming from a place of enough. I believe energy matters in relationships and the energy you're putting out there will locate a partner who has the same energy you do. If your energy is positive and open, you'll attract the same. If it's negative and needy, you'll attract that. To boost yourself in terms of energy, focus on gratitude and what's going well. Don't just think about it but feel it every day. Feel how good it is to have all the things in your life that are going well. Feel blessed, abundant and thankful.

Don't focus too much on your partner and his characteristics. Know what you're looking for but work on the part you have some control over: yourself. Take time to reflect upon your attitudes and behavior from the past relationship. Which realizations and wisdom have you acquired? What did you do in the past relationship that didn't help it or that harmed it? What do you need to work on with yourself? What do you need to speak to a therapist or professional about? Your last relationship is a mirror allowing you to visit all the things you need to work on. Examine, analyze, work on and improve those things in yourself you are not proud of.

In addition to psychological and emotional work, focus on personal growth. If you're procrastinating and not getting things done, get to the bottom of it. Find out what you value, prioritize your life, remove distractions and find the inner motivation to start doing the things you want to do. Not working on your dreams? Reflect on what your dreams are and see what's stopping you from initiating them. Figure out the next few steps you must take to achieve your dreams. Visualize yourself achieving your dream life. Don't have good habits? Start small and take little steps every day. Do something you can easily complete but make sure you get it done every day. Don't run a marathon on day one. Walk around the block every day for a month. You'll soon find the motivation to increase the distances you're walking or running.

Look at all the areas of your life from your health to your relationships. What is going well and what isn't? If you're not happy in one area of your life, figure out what's keeping you stuck. Why are you not able to get where you want to be? Of course, to know how you want to improve that aspect of your life you must go within to figure out what it is you want. What do you want your family life to look like? What do you want your spiritual life to look like? What do you want your work life to look like? Come up with a vision for each area of your life and then put together a few steps that will help you move in that direction. Again, improving your life is in your control. Changing yourself and working on yourself is all in your power.

Create and live your dream life. You don't have to wait to live or wait until you have a partner to be happy. That's the mistake many people make. You might think your life is incomplete by yourself. You might be waiting for your life to begin and that this will happen when you're in your next relationship. Here's the wakeup call: You don't need a partner to be happy or to have a fulfilled life. I know saying this is contrary to what society, the movies, and everyone in your family and society regularly tells you but it is the truth. You can be happy by yourself.

No, you don't have to believe you'll be alone forever. You don't have to settle for the single life. If you want a partner, take steps to land one but don't live in doom and gloom without a partner. You can still enjoy the life you have by doing the things you're passionate about. You can have the life you want by spending time with the people you love, giving back to the causes you care about and socializing in all your favorite spots. You can find meaning and purpose in your kids, your career, your interests or the charities you're involved with. Work on finding a partner if you want one but live like you don't need one.

Live the best life you can imagine. I believe this is the best way to attract the partner you desire. When you're living in a place of abundance, happiness and joy, you will find a partner who can enhance your life even more in all these ways. If you're living like a bitter, angry and lonely person who is in desperate need of a partner, you'll likely find someone in that space – or no one at all. The idea isn't to fake happiness and pretend you're ok when you're not. The idea is to find the tools to cultivate happiness. The idea is to create a life you enjoy and live that life every day. The idea is to find contentment and peace of mind.

Finally, the last thought I have on this is to set the intention for that ideal partner in your life and then release any attachment to the result. Yes, surrender. Let go of your desired outcome. Instead of deeply or desperately hoping and praying for a partner, let go. When you focus too much on what you want, you're focusing only on what you don't have. Instead of focusing on not having a partner and the pain that's causing you, learn to let go. Remind yourself that you can only visualize, set an intention for and take action towards finding a partner. You can take steps to find a partner and you can do so with a positive spirit but anything more is out of your control.

To surrender, do the work to find a partner. As I've spoken about in this book, make changes within yourself, visualize the person you want, know what qualities you're looking for, go out there and mingle with like-minded individuals. While you're doing all these things, have no attachment to the outcome. Don't pray, hope or plead for someone to show up in your life. Instead, cultivate gratitude and joy for your ability to live the life you want and for the experiences you're having.

Be grateful for the opportunity to meet other people and for the moments you can spend with them. Have faith that the right person will show up at the right time. Believe in universal connections and divine time. Believe that the right time will bring the right person. Again, don't harp on when or who that person is. Surrender is living and dating without expectations, demands or things working out as you desire. It's a belief that whatever comes your way comes for the highest good.

Now, go love again

Over the years, you've suffered after splitting up with your ex. You've gone through heartache, pain and even shame with your divorce or breakup. You lost everything you had. The life you knew ended when your past relationship did.

You don't have to let your past be the same as your future. I hope you've learned ways to work through your past, let go of grief, heal and come out on the other side stronger and wiser.

Your new self after divorce is smarter, stronger and wiser. You can make decisions more easily because you've been around the block. Your experience works to your advantage. You know yourself better and, hopefully, you have more clarity about who you're looking for.

Your post-breakup life can go one of two ways. You can give up and throw in the towel. You can vow to never be lovable or have the ability to love. You can be angry with your ex, your parents, your ex's parents and everyone in between. You can shoulder the heavy baggage of your past and see your future through a lens of negativity. You can let false beliefs cloud your vision. You can feel as though loving again isn't worth the effort.

I hope this book has convinced you otherwise. You don't have to remain stuck in this place you were once in. Life is too short to let grief and misery consume you. Life is too short to be single and alone. If you crave connection and love, you can still find them. You'll just need to change your attitude and acquire more wisdom in thought and more clarity in the partner you're looking for.

Your heartbreak is here to serve you. It opened your heart and soul. You've been able to access both the pain of the hurt and the light of your soul. When your heart broke open, you received a gift of sorts to access parts of yourself you never did before. After this heartbreaking, soul-crushing breakup, you can now be more in tune with your heart and spirit. You can act from this place of strength and courage.

You can show your doubters and haters that you can get back up, dust yourself off and love again. You can show your persistence, character and grit to yourself and your kids. You can show other broken-hearted people in your life that they do not have to settle after breakup and divorce.

You can wake up to a new life with a new mate! If you believe it and act on it, you'll be with a partner before you know it. You can enhance your joy, happiness and romantic life with this new partner. You will have the emotional support, friendship and companionship this new partner will bring into your life. Life will feel sweeter. You will hear the birds chirping louder.

My message to you is simple: Don't give up. Keep hope alive when it comes to love. You owe it to your heart to love again. You owe it to your life to take another chance on love. You still have so much to give, no matter where you are in life.

Keep trekking forward no matter how many times you suffer heartbreak and how reluctant you might feel about dating and meeting new people. This time around, you can love with clarity, insight and wisdom.

Cheers to new romances. Now, go love again.

In friendship,

Vishnu

Your best love visualization

I believe in the power of love and the power of visualizations. Thus, I provide this exercise for you to complete at your convenience.

Complete this exercise when you are relaxed or before you go to bed each night.

Close your eyes. Take a deep breath.

Imagine you've woken up at a beach resort. In front of you is the back of your ideal lover and partner.

This person slowly turns around and walks your way. Imagine the feelings of excitement and happiness you experience as this person walks towards you.

Feel their energy and how they make you feel.

See yourself talking to this person and what he/she says to you.

Imagine yourself calling each other sweet names.

Have a delicious, life-changing conversation with each other.

Remind each other how long you've been waiting to see each other.

Imagine the jokes, gossip and commonalities you share with each other.

Go for a walk on the beach and continue your conversation. Know that when the sun you're walking towards sets, it's time to let go and say goodbye to each other.

Once you've reached this point and the sun is setting, embrace and kiss each other.

Tell each other when you'll see each other again.

Give each other a hug and part ways. Tell each other you can't wait to see each other again.

Wake up with this energetic and positive energy.

Know that love is possible, love is close and love is near.

Go out into the world carrying this vibrational love energy – an energy that's open and welcoming of someone who is out there looking for you.

About the Author

Vishnu Subramaniam is the author of *The Self Romance Manifesto: 21 Practices to End Self Hate and Invite Love In, 10 Sacred Laws of Healing a Broken Heart,* and *Is God Listening?* Vishnu is the blogger behind the popular relationship and personal growth blog, *Vishnu's Virtues,* where he writes about overcoming heartbreak, finding your purpose and living your best life.

Vishnu also coaches people on starting over and rebuilding their lives after difficult transitions like divorces or breakups. He helps people in transition escape unfulfilling careers, discover their lives' purposes and pursue their life-long dreams. He helps people live more intentional and conscious lives.

Before writing and coaching, Vishnu practiced divorce and criminal law. While he enjoyed helping people navigate the justice system, it wasn't his true life purpose. Vishnu left the law field and pursued his calling to inspire others.

To keep up with Vishnu's weekly posts and for a free video about coming back from rock bottom, please visit his blog at www.vishnusvirtues.com.

For the Vishnu's Virtues blog:
www.vishnusvirtues.com

Vishnu on Facebook:
https://www.facebook.com/vishnusvirtues/

Vishnu on Twitter:
https://twitter.com/VishnusVirtues

Vishnu on Instagram:
https://www.instagram.com/vishnusvirtues/

Vishnu on Amazon:
https://www.amazon.com/Vishnus-Virtues/e/B00XH077L0

For constructive feedback or questions, email me at
vishnusvirtues@gmail.com

Made in the USA
Coppell, TX
13 November 2020